National Trust Diary 2011

F
FRANCES LINCOLN LIMITED
PUBLISHERS

Frances Lincoln Limited
4 Torriano Mews
Torriano Avenue
London NW5 2RZ
www.franceslincoln.com

National Trust Pocket Diary 2011
Copyright © Frances Lincoln Limited 2010
Text and photographs copyright
© 2010 National Trust (Enterprises) Limited except where indicated in the credits

Produced under Licence from The National Trust (Enterprises) Ltd.

Astronomical information © Crown Copyright. Reproduced by permission of the Controller of Her Majesty's Stationery Office and the UK Hydrographic Office (www.ukho.gov.uk)

Every effort is made to ensure calendarial data is correct at the time of the going to press but the Publisher cannot accept any liability for any errors or changes.

Maps © Maps in Minutes™ 2007. © Crown Copyright, Ordnance Survey & Ordnance Survey Northern Ireland 2006 Permit No. NI1675 & © Government of Ireland, Ordnance Survey Ireland.

All rights reserved. No part of this publication may be reproduced, stored in a retrieval system or transmitted, in any form, or by any means, electronic, mechanical, photocopying, recording or otherwise, without either prior permission in writing from the publishers or a licence permitting restricted copying. In the United Kingdom such licences are issued by the Copyright Licensing Agency, Saffron House, 6-10 Kirby Street, London EC1N 8TS

A catalogue record for this book is available from the British Library
ISBN: 978-0-7112-3099-6
First Frances Lincoln edition 2010
9 8 7 6 5 4 3 2 1

Front cover: The Herb Garden at Buckland Abbey, Devon, with the plants confined in Box-edged beds. Amongst the over 40 varieties present, is the curry plant, prominent in the foreground. (©NTPL/Andrew Butler)
Back cover: Various kitchen utensils including brass ladles and a pestle and mortar displayed on a wooden table at Saltram, Devon. (©NTPL/Andreas von Einsiedel)
Endpapers: A detail of the dutch tiles in the Kitchen at Treasurer's House, York. The tiles date from the nineteenth century and may have been installed when Frank Green restored the house in 1897. (©NTPL/John Hammond)

PICTURE CREDITS

Introduction; Week 8, March opener (bottom left); Week 13; May opener (top left); September opener (bottom left); Week 52 ©NTPL/Nadia Mackenzie; January opener (top left) ©NTPL/Joe Cornish; January opener (bottom left and right); Week 4; Week 10; September opener (right) ©NTPL/Robert Morris; Week 3; February opener (all); Week 30; August opener (right); September opener (top left); November opener (right); December opener (bottom left and right); March opener (top left and right) ©NTPL/Val Corbett; April opener (top left and right); Week 17; May opener (right); November opener (top right); December opener (top left) ©NTPL/Andrew Butler; April opener (bottom left); Week 25 ©NTPL/Ross Hoddinott; May opener (bottom left) ©NTPL/Dennis Gilbert; Week 21 ©NTPL/Ian Shaw; June opener (top left) ©NTPL/John Miller; June opener (bottom left and right) ©NTPL/Arnhel de Serra; July opener (top left); August opener (bottom left); Week 43 ©NTPL/Mike Williams; July opener (right); October opener (bottom left and right) ©NTPL/Matthew Antrobus; July opener (bottom left); Week 29; Week 36 ©NTPL/Paul Harris; August opener (top left) ©NTPL/Neil Campbell-Sharp; Week 34 ©NTPL/Stephen Robson; Week 37 ©NTPL/Nick Guttridge; October opener (top left) ©NTPL/Myles New; November opener (bottom left) ©NTPL; Week 48 ©NTPL/Layton Thompson

RECIPE CREDITS

The following recipes are taken from *The Complete Traditional Recipe Book* by Sarah Edington (National Trust Books, 2006), and are used with the kind permission of The National Trust. Text © Sarah Edington

Cock-a-Leekie Soup (Week 5); Lanhydrock Squab Pie (February); Chicken Thyme Pie (Week 14); Date and Walnut Loaf (April); Fish and Cider Casserole (Week 18); A Salad of Herbs and Flowers (Week 22); Pickled Salmon (Gravadlax) (Week 31); Erddig Apple Scones (September); Golden Cider Soup (Week 40); Piccalilli (October); Pear and Rosemary Jelly (Week 44); Christmas Pudding (Week 47); Mulled Wine (December).

The following recipes are taken from *Traditional Teatime Recipes* by Jane Pettigrew (National Trust Books, 2007), and are used with the kind permission of The National Trust. Text © Jane Pettigrew

Welsh Cakes (January); Bateman's Soda Bread (Week 9); Eighteenth-century Pepper Cake (March); Sticky Lemon Cake (May); Seventeenth-century Honey Cake (Week 26); Petworth Pudding (June); Carrot and Pineapple Cake (July); Manchester Tart (August); Blackberry Tea Bread (Week 35); Canons Ashby Coconut Cake (November); Ripon Christmas Bread (Week 53).

These books can be bought at National Trust shops and are available online at www.nationaltrustbooks.co.uk

Calendar 2011

JANUARY
M T W T F S S
            1 2
3 4 5 6 7 8 9
10 11 12 13 14 15 16
17 18 19 20 21 22 23
24 25 26 27 28 29 30
31

FEBRUARY
M T W T F S S
  1 2 3 4 5 6
7 8 9 10 11 12 13
14 15 16 17 18 19 20
21 22 23 24 25 26 27
28

MARCH
M T W T F S S
  1 2 3 4 5 6
7 8 9 10 11 12 13
14 15 16 17 18 19 20
21 22 23 24 25 26 27
28 29 30 31

APRIL
M T W T F S S
        1 2 3
4 5 6 7 8 9 10
11 12 13 14 15 16 17
18 19 20 21 22 23 24
25 26 27 28 29 30

MAY
M T W T F S S
            1
2 3 4 5 6 7 8
9 10 11 12 13 14 15
16 17 18 19 20 21 22
23 24 25 26 27 28 29
30 31

JUNE
M T W T F S S
    1 2 3 4 5
6 7 8 9 10 11 12
13 14 15 16 17 18 19
20 21 22 23 24 25 26
27 28 29 30

JULY
M T W T F S S
        1 2 3
4 5 6 7 8 9 10
11 12 13 14 15 16 17
18 19 20 21 22 23 24
25 26 27 28 29 30 31

AUGUST
M T W T F S S
1 2 3 4 5 6 7
8 9 10 11 12 13 14
15 16 17 18 19 20 21
22 23 24 25 26 27 28
29 30 31

SEPTEMBER
M T W T F S S
      1 2 3 4
5 6 7 8 9 10 11
12 13 14 15 16 17 18
19 20 21 22 23 24 25
26 27 28 29 30

OCTOBER
M T W T F S S
          1 2
3 4 5 6 7 8 9
10 11 12 13 14 15 16
17 18 19 20 21 22 23
24 25 26 27 28 29 30
31

NOVEMBER
M T W T F S S
  1 2 3 4 5 6
7 8 9 10 11 12 13
14 15 16 17 18 19 20
21 22 23 24 25 26 27
28 29 30

DECEMBER
M T W T F S S
      1 2 3 4
5 6 7 8 9 10 11
12 13 14 15 16 17 18
19 20 21 22 23 24 25
26 27 28 29 30 31

Calendar 2012

JANUARY
M T W T F S S
            1
2 3 4 5 6 7 8
9 10 11 12 13 14 15
16 17 18 19 20 21 22
23 24 25 26 27 28 29
30 31

FEBRUARY
M T W T F S S
    1 2 3 4 5
6 7 8 9 10 11 12
13 14 15 16 17 18 19
20 21 22 23 24 25 26
27 28 29

MARCH
M T W T F S S
      1 2 3 4
5 6 7 8 9 10 11
12 13 14 15 16 17 18
19 20 21 22 23 24 25
26 27 28 29 30 31

APRIL
M T W T F S S
            1
2 3 4 5 6 7 8
9 10 11 12 13 14 15
16 17 18 19 20 21 22
23 24 25 26 27 28 29
30

MAY
M T W T F S S
  1 2 3 4 5 6
7 8 9 10 11 12 13
14 15 16 17 18 19 20
21 22 23 24 25 26 27
28 29 30 31

JUNE
M T W T F S S
        1 2 3
4 5 6 7 8 9 10
11 12 13 14 15 16 17
18 19 20 21 22 23 24
25 26 27 28 29 30

JULY
M T W T F S S
            1
2 3 4 5 6 7 8
9 10 11 12 13 14 15
16 17 18 19 20 21 22
23 24 25 26 27 28 29
30 31

AUGUST
M T W T F S S
    1 2 3 4 5
6 7 8 9 10 11 12
13 14 15 16 17 18 19
20 21 22 23 24 25 26
27 28 29 30 31

SEPTEMBER
M T W T F S S
          1 2
3 4 5 6 7 8 9
10 11 12 13 14 15 16
17 18 19 20 21 22 23
24 25 26 27 28 29 30

OCTOBER
M T W T F S S
1 2 3 4 5 6 7
8 9 10 11 12 13 14
15 16 17 18 19 20 21
22 23 24 25 26 27 28
29 30 31

NOVEMBER
M T W T F S S
      1 2 3 4
5 6 7 8 9 10 11
12 13 14 15 16 17 18
19 20 21 22 23 24 25
26 27 28 29 30

DECEMBER
M T W T F S S
          1 2
3 4 5 6 7 8 9
10 11 12 13 14 15 16
17 18 19 20 21 22 23
24 25 26 27 28 29 30
31

Introduction

The National Trust was founded in 1895 by Victorian philanthropists, concerned about the impact of uncontrolled development and industrialisation, as an independent charity to preserve places of historic interest or natural beauty for the nation to enjoy forever.

More than a century later, it cares for over 300 historic houses and gardens, 49 industrial monuments and mills, nearly 650,000 acres of countryside and more than 700 miles of coastline throughout England, Wales and Northern Ireland.

From ancient stone circles and Victorian cotton mills, to gardens, village streets and castles, the Trust looks after places that connect the present and the future with the past, enabling new generations to better understand the meaning and value of our cultural heritage. It also manages the largest and most diverse collection of open space in the country: forests, woods, fens, farmland, downs, mainland, nature reserves, beaches and islands, often in areas experiencing severe pressure from new development.

The National Trust invests over £160 million a year in the nation's environmental infrastructure and is now Europe's largest voluntary organisation for nature conservation. Its unique learning programmes help both youth and adults to acquire skills that contribute to the quality of life in their local communities.

The *National Trust Diary 2011* celebrates the cultivation and preparation of food – from the humble cottage 'veg' patch to the large kitchen garden of the 'big house'. Seasonal recipes, sourced from National Trust properties, are included throughout.

Three whiteslip earthenware containers in front of a white-tiled wall edged with a floral pattern in the Dairy Scullery at Uppark, West Sussex.

Plas yn Rhiw

Pwllheli, Gwynedd

Welsh Cakes

The most famous of traditional cakes from Wales, these little flat spicy griddle cakes were offered to visitors calling at the house. Welsh cakes were traditionally cooked on a bakestone that sat on the open kitchen fire. Their name in Welsh is *pice ar y maen* which literally means 'cakes on the stone'. Two variations are cooked today – Lech Cymreig is made with plain flour to give a flatter, crisper cake, and Jam Split is made by cutting the Welsh cake across the middle and filling it with jam.

Makes 10-12 cakes
225g (8oz) self-raising flour, sifted
pinch of salt
50g (2oz) lard, softened
50g (2oz) butter, softened
75g (3oz) granulated sugar
25g (1oz) currants
½ egg, beaten
1½ tbsp milk
caster sugar for sprinkling

Preheat a griddle or a heavy fat frying pan to a moderate, even temperature. Mix together the flour and salt and rub in the fat. Add the sugar and currants and mix with the egg and milk to a soft dough. On a floured board, roll out to a thickness of 0.5-1cm (¼-½in) and cut out rounds using a 7.5cm (3in) cutter. Place on the griddle and cook both sides until light golden. Lift on to a wire rack and leave to cool. Sprinkle with caster sugar before serving.

The small manor house of Plas yn Rhiw has spectacular views across Cardigan Bay (far left, top). In the kitchen traditional weights and scales (left) sit alongside the kettle and saucepans on a Valor paraffin stove (far left, bottom).

December • January 2011

WEEK 1

27 Monday — We went to Stockton I got a skirt + blouse Mike rang Jim rang Michael we went to the Club the usual crowd were out

28 Tuesday — Jim Norton me Stockton got a skirt Mike rang about three times Mike rang said he might come on Thursday

29 Wednesday — Mike rang he's not well went doctors have to have X Ray on my spine I rang our Ada she said she feels staying in

30 Thursday — Went for my X Ray didn't have to wait very long Michael phoned twice we went to the club.

31 Friday — I went over Ada Paul gave me a gift home, rang Mike rang Ada she rang back went club David came over to wish me a happy new year.

1 Saturday — went over the shops Aunt Ada rang Mike rang I rang Mike Carl rang said they all had a good time over Christmas

2 Sunday — went to Stockton very cold went to the club it was very busy. we had rang Mike and he us.

January — WEEK 2

Monday 3 — Holiday, UK, Republic of Ireland, Canada, Australia and New Zealand
Jim went Norton I stayed in Mike rang we went to the club it was back to normal no one was out very busy

Tuesday 4 — New Moon. Holiday, Scotland and New Zealand
we went to Stockton I got a few bargains Mike rang I rang him Aunt Ada rang she's not coming out Wednesday went to the club Mike rang 11:15

Wednesday 5
We went to Stockton then Jim went to the shops I cleaned up Mike rang Jim rang Mike then Mike rang about his horses. Stayed in

Thursday 6 — Epiphany
Mike came went to the club with his dad the score 1-1 We went to Stockton Jim rang Michael then Michael rang Jim about the horses

Friday 7
Its very frosty Jim went to the shops I cleaned up Mike rang Jim went to Norton Mike rang before we went out went to the club talked to Norman & Bernie

Saturday 8
Mike rang I went to Stockton got a blouse Mike rang again went to the club Dance hall but Sue wasn't out. When we got in missed a call off Carl

Sunday 9
I did some washing they went to Stockton Mike rang I rang him before our dinner.

WEEK 3   2 wakes   £220 Bingo Jim   **January**
Mac   Carl rang

Monday 10
Jim went Shops I did the sheets Mike rang he was at Tony Jim phoned Mike before we had our teas we went to the club I got a thank you card off Heidi

Tuesday 11
We went to H.Pool I got some lights socks for Jim Mike rang I rang Aunt Ada she's not going to Stockton went to the Club

First Quarter
Wednesday 12
I cleaned up Jim's gone to Norton Mike rang went Stockton I got 2 bottles of Wisky Mac we stayed in Watched TV had a few drinks

Thursday 13
Mike came went to the Club with Jim went to Stockton put money in rang Ada Mike and Jim went out Jim Norton went to the Club Jim won £20 on the bingo very good

Friday 14
Mike rang we went to M.Bro to see Mike in the Town Mike rang us after tea went to the club

Saturday 15
Jim went Shops me Stockton got a case rang Mike Carl rang went Club Sue was out she had not been in for 9 Weeks

Sunday 16
Jim went to the Shops I washed and cleaned up

The small range in the Kitchen Scullery at Lanhydrock, Cornwall. This range was used for cooking vegetables and the stock pot was kept here.

January — WEEK 4

19th Nat Carl rang

17 Monday We went to Stockton ... a hour Mike rang I rang Mike later we went to the Cons the usual crowd were out.

18 Tuesday Jim went to Norton Mike rang Jim rang Mike before tea I rang Aunt Ada went to the club Bob and Iris and Francis allso Marie

19 Wednesday I went to Stockton with Jim I met Aunt Ada I got the bus with her and went to Ada's had my dinner Ada drove me to the bus Aunt Ada rang Mike rang our Ada rang (Full Moon)

20 Thursday Mike came went club with Jim we went to Stockton got skirt becourse Mike rang I rang him went to ~~~~~~ the club Bob and Christine Bob + Iris I phoned Carl Nat got engaged 19th

21 Friday Michael rang Jim shops stayed in very cold + frosty Mike rang twice more Berni and Norman were out Colin and Marie but Colin was on the door we sat playing cards

22 Saturday Jim went to Norton me Stockton I got some pants + tights Mike rang Carl rang went to the club Sue wasn't in but Jean and Ray were out.

23 Sunday Went to Stockton for a run out Mike rang I rang him before we had our dinner stayed in

The vegetable garden at Rosedene. Rosedene was first occupied in 1849 by early Chartists, who cultivated their own fruit and vegetables.

Cock-a-Leekie Soup

A famous old Scottish recipe, this is the alternative to Scotch Broth on Burns Night (25th January) or St. Andrew's Day (30th November). *Kettners Book of the Table* describes this as the modern version of Malachi, a fourteenth-century recipe that featured a 'Ma', the old name for a fowl or chicken. The prunes are optional but they do give the dish a distinctive flavour.

Serves 4
Leg and wing joints of 1 chicken, plus the carcass
700g (1½lb) leeks, chopped and washed
3 bacon rashers, chopped
1 mixed bunch of parsley and thyme
1 bay leaf
1.2 litres (2 pints) water
110g (4oz) stoned prunes
salt and pepper to taste

Put the chicken leg and wing joints, and the carcass, in a large pan, together with the bacon, the herbs and all but two of the leeks. Cover with the water. Bring to the boil, turn down the heat, cover the pan and simmer for at least 1 hour, until the chicken is tender. Season to taste, then strain off the liquid, picking out the chicken meat and cutting it into pieces to serve. Put the broth and the chicken pieces back in the pan together with the stoned prunes and the remaining leeks. Simmer very gently for 15 minutes and serve piping hot.

January

WEEK 5

Jim got 2 bottles wine Jodie? rang Carl not in

Monday 24
Went to put my prescription in Jim went to the Asda we went to Stockton I got a blouse & 2 skirts Mike rang we went to the club we went to the club Les Mandy Mark also the football cards were out

Tuesday 25 Burns Night
Went to H.Pool seen Mavis Mike rang went to the club on our own we talked to Marie Ann and Ken were with another couple. We rang Carl no answer

Wednesday 26 Last Quarter / Holiday, Australia (Australia Day)
Jim went Asda I went for my pills Mike rang I rang Ada Jim rang Mike he rang back I still have a headache.

Thursday 27
Mike came went club with Jim we went to Stockton after Mike went we went to the club Bob and I, my John & Val and the two girls were in

Friday 28
Mike rang Jims shops I stayed in for a change Mike rang to talk to his dad went club Norman and Bernie were out so was John Vals husband.

Saturday 29
Mike rang Jims gone shops I went to Stockton my neck hurts still Carl rang we went to the club Sue was out so was Jean and Ray + Maureen

Sunday 30
We went to Stockton I got 2 wine rang Mike he rang his dad about the horses stayed in

Lanhydrock

Bodmin, Cornwall

Lanhydrock Squab Pie

Squabs were pigeons, but as these were scarce and generally eaten by the rich, lamb has been substituted in this poor man's version. The apples and onions were used to make up for the lack of meat. In latter years the cream has been added to make the dish more special.

Serves 6 plus
700g (1½lb) stewing lamb or cooked diced lamb
450g (1lb) onions, sliced
450g (1lb) cooking apples, peeled and sliced
mixed herbs
125ml (4fl oz) vegetable stock (using a stock cube)
350g (12oz) shortcrust or puff pastry
300ml (½ pint) double cream or clotted cream
salt and pepper to taste

Preheat oven to 200°C, 400°F, gas mark 6. Arrange the meat, onions and apples in alternate layers in a pie dish. Sprinkle with mixed herbs (or just rosemary) and pour the stock over everything. Cover with the pastry and cook in the oven until the pastry is done – approximately 30 minutes. Turn the oven temperature down to 160°C, 325°F, gas mark 3, and cook for a further hour. If the pastry starts to brown too much, cover it with foil. If the meat is pre-cooked, you may need a little less time. Remove from the oven and gently lift off the pastry top. Stir in the cream and adjust the seasoning. Replace the pastry lid and reheat for a further few minutes before serving.

Lanhydrock's kitchens would have been supplied with fresh produce by the Home Farm, including milk for making into butter and cream in the Dairy Scullery (far left, top). The main Dairy (far left, bottom) had an elaborate cooling system using piped water from the hill above. Marble and slate worktops kept food cool. The Dry Larder (left) is stocked with tins and packets of food.

January • February

WEEK 6

31 Monday Still hurts my head we went to Stockton I bought a neck support but they say that they are no good Went to the club the usual crowd were out

1 Tuesday Mike rang head still hurts Jims gone to Norton Mike rang again Aunt Ada rang we went to the Club sat on our own

2 Wednesday I rang Mike head still hurts Mike rang in we went to Stockton Mike rang again we stayed in watched T.V had a bath and had a few drinks

3 Thursday Mike came went to the club with his my neck still hurts Jims gone are stops Ada rang went to the club Ann and Ken sat with another couple

New Moon
Chinese New Year

4 Friday we got the coach it was late again we were having a good run down till there was a crash so we never got to the hotel till 730 had a bath then went down for our dinner

5 Saturday we went round the shops still windy and wild we got the bus they run every few minutes then we went back to the hotel for our dinner

6 Sunday we went round the shops its still wild + windy the walk in doctors he gave me only 3 pills said I had to see my own doctor

Accession of Queen Elizabeth II
Holiday, New Zealand (Waitangi Day)

February

WEEK 7

Monday 7 — We got back 4:30 Good trip I rang Mike we went to the club my head still hurts.

Tuesday 8 — Dr rang I went for my pills Mike rang I rang Mike we went to the club sat on our own again.

Wednesday 9 — Rang Mike neck no better Jims gone to Stockton I rang Aunt Ada Mike rang Jim rang him before our tea Ada rang me we stayed in watched T.V.

Thursday 10 — Mike rang came over went to the club with Jim Head hurts still, after Mike left we went to Stockton went to the club Val came to talk to us about the holidays

First Quarter — Friday 11 — My neck still hurts Mike rang 12 o'clock went to Mgro seen Mike for a little while we went to the club sat on our own again Elvis Ann came to talk to us said it was to noisy down the dance hall

Saturday 12 — Jim went shops Mike rang neck no better Mike rang Born got beat we went to the club Sue was in with Mike we had a good night.

Sunday 13 — we went to the walk in hospital she said it would take a long time to heal up Michael phoned. We watched the Bafftas on T.V.

February — WEEK 8

I got a cat + Ada rang Carl

14 Monday — St. Valentine's Day
Jim got me a neckerace Jim's gone to the shops Mike rang we had a week down the filling station Ada rang went club Mark Les Mandy + Michael were out

15 Tuesday
Went doctors have to have a X Ray on my neck Mike rang Aunt Ada rang went out down the dance hall for a change Sue was in so was Mike had a good night

16 Wednesday
Met Aunt Ada went back to her house Mike rang Aunt Ada rang our Ada rang my neck still hurts we stayed in watched T.V. had a bath and a few drinks

17 Thursday
Did some washing my neck still hurts we went to Hartlepool Mikey rang a few times went club Bob + Jo is going + Joh were in also there too friends we had a nice time no Ann + Ken.

18 Friday — Full Moon
Jim went to Norton I went for our bill my neck still hurts Mike rang we went to the club Jo Jo and David were out David came over and talked to us not a bad night rang Ada engaged

19 Saturday
Went to Stockton Jim went to the shops Mike rang twice Ada rang Carl rang went to Club Sue + Mich were out Jim won £50 single line on the Bingo I was very unlucky

20 Sunday
We went to Stockton it's very cold + windy I did the bedrooms Mike rang we stayed and watched T.V and had a few drinks

Copper pots and pans on display in the Kitchen at Felbrigg Hall, Norfolk.

Bateman's Soda Bread

A soft, light bread, this recipe is from Rudyard Kipling's Jacobean house in East Sussex.

Makes 1 x 15cm (6in) round loaf
225g (8oz) plain wholemeal flour, sifted
2 tsp baking powder
1/2 tsp salt
1 tsp demerara sugar
25g (1oz) butter, softened
150ml (5fl oz) milk
cracked wheat, oatmeal or oats

Preheat the oven to 200°C, 400°F, gas mark 6. Grease a baking tray. Mix together the flour, baking powder, salt and sugar and rub in the butter. Add the milk and mix to a soft dough. Shape into a round and place on the prepared tray. Brush the top with a little milk and sprinkle with cracked wheat, oatmeal or oats. Bake for 20-30 minutes until well risen and browned. Remove from the oven and serve warm with plenty of butter.

WEEK 9 — Jim did my hair — **February**

Monday 21 — Holiday, USA (Washington's Birthday)
We went to the shops I got a blouse also a ironing board. Got my phone bill in. Rang Mike he rang us. Went to bed for a while. Ada rang Mike rang before we went out. Only a few in the club. My head still aching.

Tuesday 22
We went to Stockton seen Maureen Mike rang Dorothy hem. Got £100 pound out. Mike rang we went down the dance hall we had a good nite. Mike rang again before we went out.

Wednesday 23
Mike rang we went to M Bro Jim booked a holiday for Friday I rang Mike he rang us back. Mike rang again just before my bath. We stayed in watched T.V, had a bath.

Thursday 24 — Last Quarter
Mike came went club with Jim, did the washing went over the doctors then packed and did the ironing. Jim Won 2-0 Mike rang I rang Ada and Aunt Ada also Mike.

Friday 25
Holiday. We went to Stock on the bus was a little bit late we got to the hotel at 7-30 had our dinner then went for the free bar we had a good drink then went to bed nice room.

Saturday 26
We didn't go on the trip we went round the town it was very cold and windy went back to the hotel there was a good turn and free drinks all night.

Sunday 27
We got the bus to have a little ride round it was good. Then back to the hotel there was a girl called Cathrine she was very good.

February • March
WEEK 10

Carl rang Barbara rang me 3 March X Ray. Rang Carl

28 Monday
We were up at 6 o'clock got away by 8 o'clock got home 6 o'clock rang Mike Ada phoned she's in remission Mike rang 2 times went to the club good night but we were very tired

1 Tuesday — St. David's Day
Jim went and picked my pills up for me I washed and cleaned up. Mike rang Jim & Ada rang Mike again. We went Con's Sue and Mitz were out. I rang Carl talked to Heidi

2 Wednesday
Met Aunt Ada went for a cuppa then got the bus me to Ada's Michael told me how to test and I came home Mike rang Ada and he rang me when I got in. Ada rang me so did Aunt Ada stayed in watched T.V.

3 Thursday
X Ray hospital we were out in no time rang Mike he rang us he's working he went to the club with dad. After Mike went we went to Stockton got Blouse & skirt Mike rang we went to the club sat on our own again Bob +

4 Friday — New Moon
Gig + Bobs w. A rang Ada no luck Jims gone to the shops Mike rang I stayed in all day Jim rang Mike rang Mike we went to the club sat on our own talked to Berny. We came home really early had a few brandys

5 Saturday
I went to Stockton Jim N. Norton. Mike rang I rang Bros. Ada rang Mike rang Carl rang we had another call off Mike said Boro lost we went to the club Sue and Mike were out good night

6 Sunday
Mike rang. We went to Stockton Mike rang me he also said Carl rang him we had a few drinks watched the T.V.

Lemons growing on the south front of Phillipps House, set in Dinton Park, Wiltshire. Larger houses often had a glass house where exotic fruits could be cultivated.

Wordsworth House and Garden

Cockermouth, Cumbria

Eighteenth-century Pepper Cake

Although generally used in savoury dishes, black pepper is sometimes added to cakes with ginger and other spices. Some recipes for this traditional Westmorland fruit cake also add dates and walnuts but this one from Wordsworth House, the birthplace of William Wordsworth, uses cloves, currants, raisins and peel.

Makes 1 x 22.5cm (9in) round cake
450g (1lb) plain flour, sifted
1 tsp baking powder
100g (4oz) butter, softened
225g (8oz) caster sugar
100g (4oz) currants
100g (4oz) raisins
25g (1oz) mixed candied peel
1/2 tsp ground cloves
1/2 tsp ground ginger
1/2 tsp ground black pepper
225g (8oz) black treacle
2 eggs, beaten

Preheat the oven to 150°C, 300°F, gas mark 2. Grease and line a 22.5cm (9in) round deep cake tin. Mix together the flour and baking powder and rub in the butter until the mixture resembles fine breadcrumbs. Add all the other ingredients and mix to a thick batter. Turn into the prepared tin and bake for 2-2½ hours until a skewer comes out clean. Remove from the oven and leave to cool in the tin for 15 minutes before turning out on to a wire rack to cool completely. When cool, wrap in foil or cling film and store for a few days before using.

The cake may be coated with marzipan and iced with a plain white icing made with 175-225g (6-8oz) icing sugar, sifted and mixed with 1-2 tbsp cold water or lemon juice.

The kitchen garden at Wordsworth House (left). Here herbs were grown for medicinal purposes as well as for use in everyday cooking. Fresh produce would be preserved as jams, jellies and pickles for the winter months (far left, bottom). The orchard supplied fruit for eating, juicing and making cider.

March

WEEK 11

7 Monday Washed did the Ironing Lubard out Jim gone to the shops Mike rang he rang again after tea We went to the Club there was only Mandy Les Mike and the four football lads out.

8 Tuesday We went to M.Bro got some boots seen Graham. Mike rang we did the cubards Mike rang seen Stewart & Margret on the bus Cows dance hall 50 pence ticket. Mike rang again

Shrove Tuesday

9 Wednesday I went to S.tons Jim Norton got a belt skirt Mike rang missed it so I rang him. I did the cubards in the back We had a few Calls off Michael stayed in.

Ash Wednesday

10 Thursday Mike came went Club with Jim when Mike went, we went to Stockton. We went to the Club Michael phoned Bob and Iris Val and John were out we sat on our own again. Mike gave us £10 he had a win.

11 Friday Jim went to Norton I did some washing Mike rang Mike rang twice Ada rang she said she's doing fine They all went out for a meal to celebrate went Club no one in hardly sat on our own again.

12 Saturday went Stockton seen Mavis Jim Norton Mike rang I cleaned my Jewelry Mike rang again Mike rang again. went to the Club Sue and Mike were out we had a good night

First Quarter

13 Sunday I cleaned my Jewelry boxes out then we went to Stockton Michael rang three times in all We stayed in Watched T.V.

WEEK 12 — **March**

17th Carol rang Jim wishy
Tracy. Thursday 10 oclock

Commonwealth Day — Monday 14
Jim went to the shops I cleaned up went to H pool got some good bargains rang Mike he rang back we went to the club not many in only the usual came home early

Tuesday 15
Jim went to the shops I did the flower baskets Mike rang about three times Aunt Ada called phoned Ada. We went to the cons in the dance hall we had a good night watching them all dancing.

Wednesday 16
Met Aunt Ada in Stockton Jim got the bus with me to get the ironing board went to Ada's she gave me a lift to the bus Aunt Ada rang Jim got 3 bottles of whisky went to see Uncle George & Enid lovely to see them

St. Patrick's Day — Thursday 17
Holiday, Northern Ireland and Republic of Ireland
I went to see Tracy she said my BB was ok Mike came got me a Elvis mug Ada rang Mike rang, I rang Carl but no answer went to the club had a good night talked to Marie about my finger

Friday 18
Jim went to the shops Mike rang I sorted of my jewelry out Stayed in Mike rang I rang Ada she rang me back. Went to the cons no one in hardly we talked to Marie

Full Moon — Saturday 19
we went to Stockton Jim went home I stayed got a jacket + tummy trainer I did the washing Carl rang I rang Afrakin. Mike rang Ada rang back Ada rang again Lewis wants the bed Sue + Mike were out but they were fitting all night

Vernal Equinox (Spring begins) — Sunday 20
rang Mike went to H pool we did a bit of tidying up changed the blinds in Carols room and the back curtains
                                                                    Stayed in

March — WEEK 13

Doctors 4:50 21st Carl rang
Jim Quill office 2:45

21 Monday We went to Stockton didn't feel well called to the doctors for my pills got a card off Carl. I went to the doctors nearly forgot about it. Jim booked a little break to Manchester Mike rang went to the club not many in good night

22 Tuesday Changed the sheets went to Stockton got £100 out Mike rang I ironed my knees are hurting again Mike rang again. We went to the club Sue was out she has made up with Mike we had a good night

23 Wednesday Mike rang Jim got my pills for me I went to Stokn got some P.J. and Tummy T Jims gone to Stockton about the holiday. Mike rang again we stayed in had a few drinks then bed.

24 Thursday Mike came gave us £10 for our W.A. and for Mothers day two broaches and a angel magnet we went to bed Mike rang went to the club sat on our own again but talked to plenty people Mike rang 11.20 Jim not very well

25 Friday Jim gone down the village we went to Stockton it was warm then it got colder Mike rang twice I rang him. We went to the club played Bingo one drink then came home.

26 Saturday We went to Stockton Jim went to Norton Carl rang early not a lot to talk about Michael rang we went to the Club good time with Mike and Sue nicked a glass. Mike rang *Last Quarter*

27 Sunday We went to the Asda Jim still not well Mike rang Jim went to bed for a hour I rang Michael I tinned Jims hair. *British Summer Time begins*

The interior of Upton House, Warwickshire, was remodelled in 1927-9 and the china and kitchen utensils shown here are of this period.

Chicken Thyme Pie

Certain herbs have particular affinities. Thyme and chicken makes a good partnership. It rescues the chicken pie from lack of flavour while still leaving it the kind of easy, non-complicated recipe that conservative eaters like.

Serves 4
450g (1lb) shortcrust pastry
1 tbsp oil
25g (1oz) butter
1 large onion, peeled and sliced
6 large celery sticks, chopped
4 chicken breasts (1 per person), cut into thick slices
fresh or dried thyme
salt and pepper to taste
300ml (½ pint) chicken stock (make it with a stock cube if you have none fresh)
300ml (½ pint) thick white sauce made with 50g (2oz) butter, 50g (2oz) flour and 300ml (½ pint) milk (see below)

Preheat oven to 180°C, 350°F, gas mark 4. Melt the oil and butter and sauté the onion and celery until soft. Take out the vegetables and lay them in a pie dish. Sauté the sliced chicken in the same pan (add a little more oil if you need it) until nice and brown. Add it to the dish. Make the thick white sauce (see below) and then stir it in to make a good thick mixture with the chicken. Cover the pie dish with the pastry and decorate with any oddments. Make a hole in the centre to let out the steam and glaze with milk. Put it in the oven and cook for about 30–40 minutes until golden brown.

To make the white sauce
Put the milk in a pan and bring slowly to the boil. Remove from the heat. In a clean, heavy-based pan, melt the butter, stir in the flour and cook for 3 minutes. Strain the liquid through a sieve and gradually blend it into the flour and butter. Bring the mixture to the boil, stirring continuously. It should have thickened a little by now. Turn down the heat and cook it gently, still stirring. The harder you stir, the smoother the sauce.

WEEK 14

~~Mar 28~~ Carl phoned 4:45

March • April

Monday 28
I got a card off Aunt Ada Jims still full of cold I packed. Jim went to the shops, Mike rang, Jim cut the grass I cleaned up rang Aunt Ada. Went to the club had a good night.

Tuesday 29
Got the bus to Manchester three hour free bar Jims chest is still very chesty

Wednesday 30
We went to the walk in clinic and the Dr. gave him a good going over 5 days crash course he's been tired all the time and I hope the pills do him good.

Thursday 31
We left at 1 o'clock got home about five rang Mike he rang back we stayed in because we didn't get much sleep in the hotel to hot

Friday 1
Jim went to Norton I washed and ironed Mike rang I rang Ada Mike rang Jim I didn't go out. Mike rang we went to the club not a lot of people in John sat with us to play bingo Mike rang

Saturday 2
We got the bus together Jim to Norton me to Stockton I seen Mark & Mandy. Mike rang he's been back with Sue for 18 mth Aunt Ada rang went to the club seen Denny sat with Sue and Mick good night

Sunday 3
New Moon
Mother's Day, UK

Mike rang 11:30 washed then we went to Stockton Carl rang they are all o.k.

Stayed in watched T.V.

Cotehele

Nr Saltash, Cornwall

Date and Walnut Loaf
This Cornish recipe from Cotehele is typical in its use of spices, brown sugar and exotic fruit. From the seventeenth century, ships from the Orient imported such luxuries through the Cornish ports and many cake recipes from the region include ginger, cinnamon, nutmeg, dried dates and raisins. Cotehele would certainly have known about such ingredients, sitting as it does close to the River Tamar which for centuries was the only effective route to the outside world. The immense oven in the north wall of the kitchen almost certainly baked a number of these loaves over the centuries.

Makes 1 x 900g (2lb) loaf
225g (8oz) self-raising flour, sifted
50g (2oz) whole walnuts
1 tsp mixed spice
75g (3oz) butter, softened
100g (4oz) light or dark soft brown sugar
225g (8oz) whole dates
150ml (5fl oz) water
2 eggs, beaten
2 tbsp sesame seeds

Preheat the oven to 180°C, 350°F, gas mark 4. Grease and line a 900g (2lb) loaf tin. Mix together the flour, walnuts and mixed spice. Place the butter, sugar, dates and water in a pan and bring gently to the boil. Remove from the heat and cool for a few minutes. Add to the flour, spice and nuts with the beaten eggs and beat well. Turn into the prepared tin, hollow the middle a little and sprinkle the top with sesame seeds. Bake for 1–1¼ hours until a skewer comes out clean. Remove from the oven and turn out on to a wire rack to cool. It is delicious served sliced with butter.

The restored Tamar sailing barge "Shamrock" moored alongside the Quay at Cotehele (far left, top). The thriving Cornish sea trade would have kept Cotehele supplied with goods from far-flung places. The house would also have made the most of home-grown fruit and vegetables grown in the orchard and garden (far left, bottom, and left).

April

WEEK 15

(top scribbles) 9 rang Carl / Carl rang

4 Monday
Phoned Mike we went to Stockton. raining but we missed the drops Mike rang his dad went to the club she FB Lady in also, her + Mark no Mandy

5 Tuesday
we went to the Town centre Mike rang phoned Ada going to see her and Aunt Ada went to the club Sue was out but she was in the car go went eavy

6 Wednesday
we got the bus to Stockton Jim got the chicken I met Aunt Ada then got the bus with her to see Ada she looked fine, got home 6 o'clock Ada rang

7 Thursday
Mike came went cons with Jim I went for my pills seen Dave and Marie Ada rang as the bath rang back didnt answer but she rang back went to the Club.

8 Friday
Jim went to the doctors his sent him for a X Ray rang Mike Mike rang his dad Jim said he thinks everything ok. went to the doctor for my cream Mike rang again.

9 Saturday
Mike rang we got the bus Jim to Norton me Stockton. Mike rang we went to the Club Sue was out we had a good night Carl rang going to Israel Denny

10 Sunday
Said goodbye Rang Carl Mike rang we went to K.Pool Ada Rang Mike rang

WEEK 16 Me 2 Wishys   Sue Fri   Jims Paid £7   **April**
First Quarter Jim 2 Wishys   Carl rang
We went to the doctors but the _____ Monday 11
Pills weren't ready Mike rang Three times Jim
rang Mike before tea we went to the Club
won 50 pence on the Crickets not many in

Jim went to the doctors I cleaned up we ____ Tuesday 12
went to M'bro Mike rang I rang him back
Mike rang three times more Boro 3-3
Went down the dance Hall good night

Met Aunt Ada Jim went to Norton ____ Wednesday 13
Mike rang he rang again to talk to his dad
Aunt Ada phoned. I rang Mike he's watching
the football

Mike came went out with his dad after ____ Thursday 14
he went we went to SKF to pay my holiday
bill Mike rang his dad Mike rang me
we went to the Club Bob Iris John Joy + her sister

I rang Mike he's going to the doctors he rang ____ Friday 15
me back Sue cut our hair. I rang Aunt
Ada Jims gone to the shops went to the club
talked to Marie + Janette

I went to Stockton seen Mavis on the bus ____ Saturday 16
Mike rang Carl rang 1st Mike rang again Jim
2 Wishys Norton Mike rang went the Club
Mik and Sue were out good time we
had some food.

Palm Sunday Mike rang we went to the Asda I ____ Sunday 17
sat in the garden for a while Mike
rang again We had a lie down Mike
                                    Rang
Mike rang again

April — WEEK 17

Jims ok Doctor said he's fit for his age rang Carl.

18 Monday — Full Moon
Mike rang we got a card off Carl / Heidi Mike rang again we went to Stockton I washed my hair we went to the club the usual crowd were out

19 Tuesday — First Day of Passover (Pesach)
Mike rang twice we went over for our pills then Jim went to Norton. Jim rang Mike before tea we went to the Cons Sue was out we had a good night

20 Wednesday
We went to the hospital Mike rang six times we called to Stockton rang Mike we went to H.Pool Mike rang again Aunt Ada rang Mike rang stayed watched TV

21 Thursday — Birthday of Queen Elizabeth II, Maundy Thursday
Michael came went to the club with his dad brought me a big box of Milk Tray we got a lawn mower and he cut the grass front + back Mike rang Phoned Carl + Heidi they are all right.

22 Friday — Good Friday, Holiday, UK, Canada, Australia and New Zealand
We did the windows Mike rang we went down the E.Park seen some Canada Geese + baby ones Ada rang Mike rang went to the club David came to talk to us

23 Saturday — St. George's Day, Holiday, Australia
Jim went to Norton + to S.Tom. Mike rang Carl rang I was in the bath so never spoke to him went to the club Sue and Mike were out Ann said hello.

24 Sunday — Easter Day
Mike rang we went down the E.Park for a walk out, Mike rang again he's going to the pub

Celery 'Galaxy' growing in the Kitchen Garden at Trengwainton Garden, Cornwall.

Fish and Cider Casserole

This casserole uses coley, which makes a good substitute for cod and haddock, both of which are under threat from over-fishing. This recipe comes from the cooks at Fountains Abbey, North Yorkshire, the spectacular ruin of a great Cistercian monastery. The choir monks who lived here led lives of rigorous simplicity, with seven services of prayers every day and only the sick ate 'the meat of quadrupeds'. Fish must have been a welcome treat when it appeared on the frugal daily menu.

Serves 6
700g (1½lb) coley fillets
300ml (½ pint) vegetable stock
1 onion, peeled and sliced
50g (2oz) butter
50g (2oz) plain flour
300ml (½ pint) cider
2 tsp anchovy essence
1 tbsp lemon juice
salt and pepper to taste

For the Topping
225g (8oz) cooked potatoes, peeled and sliced
225g (8oz) apples, peeled and sliced
25g (1oz) butter

Preheat oven to 150°C, 300°F, gas mark 2. Poach the coley in the stock until cooked, approximately 10 minutes. Set aside while you make the sauce. Sauté the onion in the butter until cooked but not coloured. Stir in the flour and cook gently for a further 5 minutes. Stir in the cider, anchovy essence and lemon juice. Then use as much of the stock as you wish to make the sauce thick, but not too thick. Divide the coley fillets into six portions and place in a gratin dish. Pour over the cider sauce, coating the fish evenly. Cover with foil and place it in the oven to keep warm while you prepare the topping.

At this point, preheat the grill. Melt the extra 25g (1oz) of butter in a frying pan and gently fry the cooked potato and the apple slices for a few minutes. Arrange them on the top of the dish to cover the fish mixture completely. Then pop the dish under the grill for 5 minutes to brown the top before serving.

WEEK 18 — April • May

Carl rang Jim got 2 wine Doctors 3-20 Tues £90 on the tickets

Monday 25 — Last Quarter / Easter Monday / Holiday, UK (exc. Scotland), Republic of Ireland, Australia and New Zealand / Anzac Day (Australia and New Zealand)

We went to S-ton. Mike rang about 6 times. We went to the club most of the bar maids Mandy Les Mark & Michael were in

Tuesday 26 — Holiday, Australia (Anzac Day) (subject to confirmation)

We went to S-ton I rang Mike went to the doctors Our Ada rang Aunt Ada rang Mike rang twice more went to the club Sue was out good night

Wednesday 27

I met Aunt Ada in S-ton after shopping we went to the church for a cuppa Mike rang Jim's gone the shops. Aunt Ada phoned so did our Ada and Michael. Mike rang later

Thursday 28

Mike come went club with Jim we won £5 on the tickets we went to S-ton Mike rang we went to the club good night Bob Iris John Val & her sister were out

Friday 29

Mike rang Carl rang Jim's gone to the Town centre Watching the Royal Wedding Mike rang we went to the club not many in. Mike rang

Saturday 30

We went to S-ton Mike rang twice Mike rang twice again we went to the club Mick and Sue were out good night all told

Sunday 1

We went to the Asda seen Mike rang Carol she moves to Durham on Thurs Carl phoned Mike rang again and again

Castle Drogo

Drewsteignton, Devon

Sticky Lemon Cake

This wonderfully tangy cake is made to a recipe from Castle Drogo in Devon which was built by Julius Drewe in 1900 to Sir Edwin Lutyens' design. Mr Drewe opened his own tea store (The Willow Pattern Tea Store) in 1878, then set up the Home and Colonial Stores in 1883 and sold so much tea that he became a millionaire. While he lived at Castle Drogo, tea was served each day in the library and was a 'wonderful meal with wafer-thin bread and butter, scones and jam and Devonshire cream – and cakes in great variety, followed by whatever fruit was in season.'

Makes 1 x 17.5cm (7in) round cake
For the Cake
100g (4oz) butter, softened
100g (4oz) caster sugar
2 eggs
100g (4oz) self-raising flour, sifted
grated rind and juice of half a lemon
1½ tbsp icing sugar, sifted

For the Icing
50–75g (2–3oz) icing sugar, sifted
juice and finely grated rind of half a lemon

Preheat the oven to 160°C, 325°F, gas mark 3. Grease and line a 17.5cm (7in) round tin. Beat together the butter and sugar until light and fluffy. Beat in the eggs, one at a time, whisking hard after the addition of each one. Fold in the flour and rind, mix well and turn into the prepared tin. Bake for 45 minutes until a skewer comes out clean. Remove from the oven and make several holes in the top of the cake with a skewer. Mix together the icing sugar and lemon juice and pour over the cake. Leave in the tin until absolutely cold. Meanwhile make the icing. Mix together the icing sugar, lemon rind and juice. When the cake is cold, turn out and ice with the prepared mixture.

The oak table and cupboards in the Butler's Pantry (far left, bottom) were designed by the architect of the house, Sir Edwin Lutyens, and made by Dart and Francis in 1927. The view from the gateway and path (left) is towards Dartmoor.

May — WEEK 19

I rang Carl

2 Monday we went to H.Pool M— rang while we were out I rang Mike Rang I phoned Ada she's O.K. we went to the club not many people out

3 Tuesday we went to Stockton Mike rang I rang Mike. Michael phoned just after my bath. We went to the club down the dance HALL. Jim rang Michael *(New Moon)*

4 Wednesday I did the streets Jim went to the Town centre I rang Mike. We went to S.Ton to the M.Hole got a extra day Mike rang after tea I rang Aunt Ada. Mike rang again

5 Thursday Mike came went to the club with Jim after Mike went we went to S.Ton Mike got me a £ purely D.V.D. Mike rang after our bath we went to the club Sat on our own again.

6 Friday we went to Norton I got £50 cash back. Mike rang. rang Mike before tea. Mike rang Jim about the Boro. we went to the cons. John came to play bingo with us.

7 Saturday went to S.Ton M.Day Carl off Carl + Heidi I got my ring at last Mike rang and again I rang Carl Heidi answered Carl out with Heidi Carl rang 8.10 went the club Sue + Mich were'n Mike rang 11.15

8 Sunday Carl off Carl + Heidi we went to H.Pool Mike rang while we were out he rang again when we got in Mike rang he's going swimming Monday *(Mother's Day, USA, Canada, Australia and New Zealand)*

WEEK 20   13th May Folkstone + Bruges 4 days.   **May**

Monday 9
went to Stockton Mike rang I rang
Mike he's allright now Jim rang Mike
we went to the Club Mandy Les Mark
Jeanette and the lads were out.

Tuesday 10 — First Quarter
Mike rang Jim's gone to Norton
I cleaned up Aunt Ada rang Our Ada rang
she said she's all clear. Mike rang
we went with Lori down the dance hall

Wednesday 11
I met Aunt Ada at S. Tom went for
a cuppa in the church seen Mavis Mike
rang he's been to York races he shared a
£125 with Duncan. Aunt Ada rang

Thursday 12
Mike came gone to the club with his
dad I packed. went to the Club
Val John + our sister Bob and Iris
came home watch T.V.

Friday 13
we got the bus to Stockton the
bus was on time got to the hotel at
5.45 met 2 sisters Sue + Ann Marie
and we got some free drinks

Saturday 14
We went to Belgium on the Ferry
I got my cigs the weather was
nice it didn't rain back to the hotel
more free drinks

Sunday 15
we went to Canterbury for
the day went in a church got
tea and cakes back to the hotel
no drinks free the girls have gone home

May — WEEK 21

29 mon 3 from rang Ada, rang Carl

16 Monday We came home good trip got home about 4:30 rang Mike he rang us back twice we went to the club only Mark Lee Mike and Mandy in

17 Tuesday (Full Moon) I did the washing Jim went to the Town Centre we went to bed for a few hours Mike rang twice went to the Club down the dance hall

18 Wednesday Jim went to the T. Centre I cleaned up we went to Sion I rang Ada Mike rang I rang Mike Michael phoned we stayed in watched two good films on T.V.

19 Thursday Mike came over Jim went for our pills they both went to the Cons for snooker Mike won 2-0 went to Sion got myself a top. Went the Club Phoned Carl.

20 Friday Phoned Mike he phoned back Jim gone to Norton. Jim phoned Mike we went to the Club not very many people out. Mike rang Dillon staying over

21 Saturday Carl Holy, Mike rang Jim went to the shops I went to Stockton Mike rang before tea we went to the Club Sue or Mike weren't out. We sat on our own.

22 Sunday We went to Stockton Mike rang when we were out. Mike rang I had a good night at the Club last I rang Mike didn't answer he rang me back spoke to his dad

Wild onions growing at Llanerchaeron, an eighteenth-century estate, near Aberaeron, where they produce home-grown fruit, vegetables and herbs in the walled garden.

A Salad of Herbs and Flowers

This recipe for an Elizabethan salad comes from *The Good Huswife's Jewell* by Thomas Dawson, published in 1596. At Oxburgh House, a fortified manor dating back to the fifteenth century, this salad was made as part of an Elizabethan banquet held in the spring. It consisted of Welsh onions, shallots, sage, rosemary, thyme, parsley, chives and bay garnished with cowslips, primroses and violets, all from the garden. Only the eggs were not home-produced!

'Take your herbs and pick them very fine into fine water, and pick your flowers by themselves and wash them clean, then swing them in a strainer, and when you put them into a dish, mingle them with cucumbers or lemons pared and sliced, also scrape sugar, and put in vinegar and oil, then throw the flowers on top of the salad, and of every sort of the aforesaid things and garnish the dish about, then take the eggs boiled hard, and lay about the dish and upon the salad.'

May

WEEK 22

Monday 23 — Holiday, Canada (Victoria Day)
Jim went to the Town Centre I did the washing & ironing Mike rang Mike rang his dad about the Bee Gees Mike rang I was in the bath we went to the club

Tuesday 24 — Last Quarter
Jim went to Norton I cleaned up Mike rang we went to Mb to see Mike for a little while Mike rang before tea we went to the club in the dance hall

Wednesday 25
I met Aunt Ada in Stockton we went to the Thirty for a cuppa then we went to Invicity I went to Ada's she went home I rang Mike his got a slipped disc Aunt Ada rang Mike rang again

Thursday 26
Mike rang Sunday he came over he went to the club with his dad Mike 2-1 we went to Stockton Mike rang about the horses we went to the Corn Bol I vis John Val & her 2 sisters were in

Friday 27
Jim went shops I cleaned up we went to H.Pool Mike rang while we were out I rang Mike before we had our teas went to the club came home early Mike phoned.

Saturday 28
Jim went to Norton I Stockton Mike rang Mike rang again went Club Sue wasn't in but Mick did came home early Mike rang he won £10 on the football

Sunday 29
Jim went to the Town centre I did some washing Mike rang we went to Stockton we didn't stay long Mike rang again Jim rang Mike Mike rang again

Petworth House and Park

Petworth, West Sussex

Petworth Pudding
This recipe was found in the archives of Petworth House, although it cannot be very old as the ingredients include digestive biscuits which date back to the 1920s.

Makes 16 fingers
100g (4oz) butter
100g (4oz) granulated or caster sugar
25g (1oz) cocoa powder, sifted
1 egg
225g (8oz) digestive biscuits, crushed
50g (2oz) raisins or sultanas
50g (2oz) dark chocolate
50g (2oz) walnuts, chopped, or 50g (2oz) shredded coconut
50g (2oz) glacé cherries, roughly chopped

Grease a 17.5 x 27.5cm (7 x 11in) Swiss roll tin. Melt the butter and sugar in a medium-sized pan. Beat in the cocoa powder and the egg. Stir in the crushed biscuits and raisins or sultanas and turn into the prepared tin. Press down well and smooth the top with a palette knife. Melt the chocolate and pour over the top. Mix together the walnuts or coconut and cherries and sprinkle over the chocolate. Place the tin in the refrigerator and leave to set. When cold, cut into fingers.

Petworth House (far left, top). The west front of Petworth House was re-built between c.1688 and 1702 by the 6th Duke of Somerset. The Still Room (left), was traditionally where medicines, drinks and jams were prepared. In the Kitchen copper saucepans are stored on a dresser (far left, bottom).

May • June

WEEK 23

Ada rang wishing me Carl rang

30 Monday — Spring Bank Holiday, UK / Holiday, USA (Memorial Day)
We went to the Asda Mike rang about four times in all our Ada phoned went to the Con not many in

31 Tuesday
Mike rang seen him in Stob got for very long he went in the Betting shop. Mike rang we went to the Club. Dance Hall

1 Wednesday — New Moon
Jims went Norton Mike rang we went to Stockton its warm but very windy. Jim rang Michael Mike rang his dad. Mike rang won £300 odd pounds

2 Thursday — Ascension Day / Coronation Day
Mike came he gave us £5 each they have gone to play snooker score 1 all we went to S Ton got bottle whisky Mike rang he's won some more money

3 Friday
Hot over Mike rang. We went to Sexton brew + H.Pool. Mike rang he's going to a party went to the Club not many in so we came home after the bingo

4 Saturday
Jim went to the T. Centre I went to S.Ton. Mike rang me out he rang again later. we went to the Club in the dance hall

5 Sunday
Mike rang wanted us to meet but its to cold we went to the Asda got some money out I rang Mike Michael rang 11-45 talked to Jim.

WEEK 24   Carl rang 11th June   **June**

Holiday, Republic of Ireland
Holiday, New Zealand (The Queen's Birthday) — **Monday 6**

We went to Stockton & bought Sam a shoe, Mike rang 4:30 Duncan phoned for Michael's number. We went to the Club

Tuesday 7
Mike rang Jim went to Norton I stayed in went to the Club phoned Carl Heidi Gleda Tiffany

Feast of Weeks (Shavuot) — **Wednesday 8**
I met Aunt Ada at S.Ton saw Mavis on bus Mike rang and he rang again ~~won~~ on a horse Aunt Ada called Mike rang again + again

First Quarter — **Thursday 9**
Mike came over ~~went to the Club~~ with Dad, After Mike went we went over to pick our tablets up then we went to M.Bro. went to the Club.

Friday 10
Jim went to the B.day I cleaned up I rang Mike we went to S.Ton seen Sue's friend Midz went the Club came home very early

The Queen's Official Birthday (subject to confirmation) — **Saturday 11**
Jim went to Norton I went to S.Ton. We rang Mike for his B.Day. Carl rang. Ada rang. We went to Club Sue was in Mike rang before we went out

Whit Sunday (Pentecost) — **Sunday 12**
Washed + ironed went to S.Ton Mike rang while out rang Mikes Graham get Mike to his dinner

June — WEEK 25

Carl left mess Ada rang twice £105 Won 18 June

13 Monday — Holiday, Australia (The Queen's Birthday)
I did the streets and gone then we went to H Pool Mike rang when we got back, Ada ranging we went to the club home early

14 Tuesday
Mike rang Jim went to the Town Centre I to S.Ton. Mike rang again we went to the cons down the dancehall Mike rang late on about 1300

15 Wednesday — Full Moon
We went to North Tees Jim had a X-Ray seen Sue, we met at Folkstone Mike rang twice.

16 Thursday
Mike came wasn't here long and he took the huff and went. Jim and I went to Stockton. Went to the club

17 Friday
We went to the Asda Michael hasn't phoned yet Jim rang Mike we went to the club not a lot in Mandy was Mike came in

18 Saturday
I went to Stockton Jim went to Norton Mike rang while I was out Mike rang me 5-o'clock I won 105 pounds on the Flyer, Mike rang he rang Carl

19 Sunday — Father's Day, UK, Canada and USA / Trinity Sunday
Went to S.Ton Mike rang twice it poured down bus was twenty mins late Carl left a message on the phone we missed the call Ada rang

Buff-tailed bumble bee (*Bombus terrestris*) in flight at Trelissick Garden, Cornwall.

Seventeenth-century Honey Cake

It is thought that a daily dose of honey helps to boost the body's supply of beneficial antioxidants that protect us against age-related diseases. Tea is also a source of antioxidants and offers protection against certain cancers and heart disease. So a slice of this honey cake with two or three cups of tea will not just taste good – it will do you good as well.

Makes 1 x 900g (2lb) loaf or 17.5cm (7in) round cake
For the Cake
175g (6oz) butter, softened
175g (6oz) caster sugar
3 eggs, beaten
175g (6oz) white or wholemeal self-raising flour, sifted
1 tsp baking powder
1 tbsp clear honey
a few drops of almond essence

For the Topping
1 dessertspoon clear honey
juice of 1 lemon

For the Icing
150g (5oz) cream cheese
juice of half a lemon
175g (6oz) icing sugar, sifted

Preheat the oven to 180°C, 350°F, gas mark 4. Grease and line a 900g (2lb) loaf or a 17.5cm (7in) round tin. Beat together the butter and sugar until light and fluffy. Add the eggs, flour and baking powder and beat hard. Add the honey and almond essence and continue beating for 1-2 minutes. Turn into the prepared tin and back for 1-1¼ hours until a skewer comes out clean. (After half an hour, cover the top with a double layer of greaseproof paper as the cake tends to darken quite quickly.) Remove from the oven. Mix together the honey and lemon juice and pour over the top. Leave to cool in the tin, then turn out. Beat together the cream cheese, lemon juice and icing sugar and spread over the cooled cake. Make a pattern with the prongs of a fork and serve.

WEEK 26 — June

rang Ada not in Carl rang Thurs Jim wong 70 Ada rang

Monday 20
We went to Hartlepool we didn't get a lot Mike had rang so I gave him a buzz when we came in. Mike rang before we went out.

Tuesday 21 — Summer Solstice (Summer begins)
We went to Ston. Mike rang we were out so I rang him Mike rang. We went to the club Booked a holiday 4th July

Wednesday 22
I met Aunt Ada in Stockton we went for a cuppa in the church. Stayed in Aunt Ada rang & Michael rang

Thursday 23 — Last Quarter, Corpus Christi
Mike came over went to play snooker score 1-1 when Mike went we went to Stockton. We went to the club.

Friday 24
Went over for our bills saw Ann Graham Jim was painting Michael phoned Jim won £70 on the flyer

Saturday 25
I phoned Michael went to Stockton I had the runs very bad Carl rang I never spoke to him Ada rang

Sunday 26
We went to Stockton its very hot Mitze rang we were out Mike rang again and again

East Riddlesden Hall

Keighley, West Yorkshire

Carrot and Pineapple Cake

English recipes have included carrots in sweet dishes and cakes since medieval times but carrot cakes became particularly popular at teatime in the 1960s. This one is made to a recipe from East Riddlesden Hall where the drawing room has on show a most unusual teapot in the form of a Chinese peach-shaped wine ewer. It is a 'Cadogan teapot' named after the Honourable Mrs Cadogan who brought it to England. It has no lid but fills from the bottom through a long internal tube that runs upwards into the pot and stops the tea from flowing out again.

Makes a 1 x 900g (2lb) loaf
225g (8oz) rice flour
200g (7oz) caster sugar
½ tsp salt
½ tsp bicarbonate of soda
100g (4oz) undrained crushed pineapple
200g (7oz) grated carrot
100ml (4fl oz) corn or vegetable oil
2 eggs, beaten
½ tsp vanilla essence
50g (2oz) walnuts, roughly chopped

Preheat the oven to 190°C, 375°F, gas mark 5. Grease and line a 900g (2lb) loaf tin. Mix together the flour, sugar, salt and bicarbonate of soda. Add the pineapple, carrot, oil, eggs, vanilla essence and walnuts and mix thoroughly. Turn into the prepared tin and bake for 1–1½ hours until a skewer comes out clean. Remove from the oven and leave to cool in the tin for a few minutes before turning out on to a wire rack to cool completely.

The rear porch of East Riddlesden Hall (left), with the rose window and pinnacle. Oatcakes are a traditional northern food and the metal oatcake roller (far left, top) is from the Kitchen. The grooves in the roller prevent the mixture sticking.

June • July — WEEK 27

rang Care.

27 Monday We went over the chemist for Jims pills he had been to Norton then we went to Stockton its realy very hot rang Mike

28 Tuesday Its not so very hot today Mike rang he rang twice more he rang at 11-30 about the horses.

29 Wednesday Met Aunt Ada in Stockton Jim is doing the painting Michael rang Aunt Ada rang Mike rang about to mow Kumer

30 Thursday Mike came over went to the cows with his dad We went to Stockton I phoned Mike when we got in

1 Friday Jim rang Mike to say we aunt going on Sun Mike rang later Jims gone to the Town centre Mike rang about three times in all

New Moon
Holiday, Canada (Canada Day)

2 Saturday I went to Stockton Jim went to Norton I rang Mike went to the Club Phoned Care when we got home upstairs

3 Sunday Mike rang cleaned ~~the~~ Went to Stockton very hot Mike rang again Rang Ada not in

WEEK 28 — July

a day's Liver Care rang

Monday 4 — Holiday, USA (Independence Day)
We went to Stockton got the coach there called in at the war museum got to the hotel round four, had a bath went for our dinner

Tuesday 5
We went to Chester bit tiring walking round all the shops then back to hotel.

Wednesday 6
Went to Liverpool it was a good day had a ride on the bus went to the Adelphi hotel we stayed at last year

Thursday 7
Came away from the hotel at 10.00 went to the Trafford centre very boring we have been a few times before

Friday 8 — First Quarter
Jim went to Norton I did the washing and ironing then after lunch we went to Stockton Mike rang twice

Saturday 9
We went to Stockton met Mike Jim went home and I stayed with Mike. Went club Carl rang Louis it went off I rang him A. Machin

Sunday 10
Mike rang we went to Stockton gareth's mam next door we were talking to.

WEEK 29 — July

Phoned Carol. rang Ada Jodys Wine

Monday 11
Went to get my feet done took my prescription over as well got soaked coming home Mike rang I rang him. Went to the club

Tuesday 12
Holiday, Northern Ireland (Battle of the Boyne)
Mike rang Jim went to Morton & ironed his new shirts we went to the club I phoned Carol when we got home

Wednesday 13
We went to Stockton after Mike rang went over for my tablets we stayed in Mike rang again

Thursday 14
Mike came over went to the club to play snooker Phoned Ada went club christen Bob & Js Bob Val & sisters + Bob were out

Friday 15
Full Moon / St. Swithin's Day
Jim went to the Town Centre we went to Stockton very warm Mike rang got some more pills we went to the Club Berry and Norman were out

Saturday 16
I rang Mike very wet I got a bottle Vodka wine Jim rang Michael he said he was going to a Rock & Roll night.

Sunday 17
I rang Mike we went to Stockton it never stopped raining on and off all day

Sweet pea (*Lathyrus odoratus*) growing in the walled kitchen garden at Knightshayes Court, Tiverton, Devon.

July — WEEK 30

Carl's B-Day. Carl rang

18 Monday Mike rang we were in bed we went to H.Poole it was very heavy rain but missed most of it. We went to the club the lads in + Mark Lee Mandy rang Carl

19 Tuesday Jim went to the Town Centre I cleaned up. Michael phoned he's been swimming we went to the club down the dance hall

20 Wednesday Jim came to stop with me I met aunt Ada Mike rang before we went. We went to the B.Shop Mike wasn't in went to Ada's she gave me a lift home

21 Thursday I did the sheets phoned Michael we went to Stockton I paid for a holiday 29th July to Cambridge + Lowdy went to the cons

22 Friday Michael phoned he was very sleepy We went to M.Bar Mike wasn't in Graham never seen Mike rang 5:15 him

23 Saturday Mike rang I went to Stockton Jim the Town Centre. Carl rang went to the club won £20 on the tote   *Last Quarter*

24 Sunday Mike rang we did the curtains then to the Asda rang aunt Ada rang Ada Mike rang again

Victorian ice-cream making equipment in the Dairy at Ham House, Richmond-upon-Thames.

Pickled Salmon (Gravadlax)

Pickling in salt was one method used not only for fish but also for meat to keep it through the lean winter months. This recipe is practical but also delicious, particularly if you use fresh dill. The salty, aromatic fish makes a perfect appetiser. Very good for entertaining too – the work, such as it is, has been done days before it is needed.

Serves 4
450g (1lb) fresh salmon fillet, skinned
coarse-grain mustard
1 packet fresh dill, finely chopped (dried dill can be used)
rock salt
freshly ground pepper to taste
lemon wedges

Ask the fishmonger for a cut from the thick end of the fillet, and allow approximately 50g (2oz) of salmon per serving. Start this dish at least three days before you wish to serve it.

   Cut a piece of clingfilm large enough to wrap the salmon in. Scatter a thick layer of rock salt on the clingfilm. Spread both sides of the salmon first with coarse-grain mustard, then with the dill, to cover the fish completely. Wrap the salmon in the clingfilm, then wrap the parcel in foil and chill for at least 3 days, turning from time to time. You can leave it to pickle for 7 days. It is not necessary to unwrap the fish.

   To serve, remove the foil and clingfilm, slice the salmon thinly, garnish with lemon wedges and serve with brown bread and butter, a little green frisée and some Dill Mayonnaise.

phoned Care Tuesday

WEEK 31
July

Monday 25
Went to the doctors then we went to Stockton I got pain shoes + a blouse Mike rang Mike he said hid rang Back later. never did

Tuesday 26
Mike rang we were going to Skeg but ended up at Norton there was a travel hold up, a lorry overturned on the A19.

Wednesday 27
we went to Stockton Michael phoned he had been to see Mary in Stockton.

Thursday 28
Michael came went to the club with Dad, We went to Stockton I got a blouse

Friday 29
The coach was late again we stopped off at Stamford then we went to the hotel very nice a new one

Saturday 30
New Moon
We had a trip to Cambridge it was very busy we saw a wedding which was very nice went Hotel after dinner went to a night club

Sunday 31
we went to Hingham and Spalding it was good the weather was very wind to us

Dunham Massey

Altrincham, Cheshire

Manchester Tart

This meringue-topped tart is a little like a Queen of Puddings in a pastry shell. The recipe comes from Dunham Massey where the 'tearoom' in the house holds rare tea and coffee tables, the family silver teawares and two tall tea caddies of japanned metal inlaid with mother of pearl. These large tins would have held the main supply of loose-leaf tea and smaller caddies, now on show on side tables and mantel shelves in the drawing and dining rooms, would have been regularly replenished.

Makes 1 x 20cm (8in) round tart
175g (6oz) flaky pastry
3-4 tbsp raspberry or strawberry jam
rind of 1 lemon, cut into strips
300ml (10fl oz) milk
50g (2oz) fresh breadcrumbs
50g (2oz) butter, softened
2 eggs, separated
75g (3oz) caster sugar
1 tbsp brandy
caster sugar for dredging

Make or buy the flaky pastry and chill for at least 45 minutes. Preheat the oven to 190°C, 375°F, gas mark 5. Grease and line a 20cm (8in) round pie dish or loose-bottomed round tin. On a floured board, roll out the pastry and use to line the prepared tin. Spread the jam over the base. Put the lemon rind and milk into a pan and bring to the boil. Remove from the heat and strain on to the breadcrumbs. Leave to stand for 5 minutes. Add the butter, egg yolks, 25g (1oz) of the sugar and the brandy and beat well. Pour into the pastry case and bake for 45 minutes. Meanwhile whisk the egg whites until stiff and fold in the remaining 50g (2oz) of the sugar. Remove the tart from the oven and spread the meringue over the filling. Dredge with caster sugar and bake for a further 15 minutes until the meringue is brown. Remove from the oven and leave to cool. Serve cold with fresh cream.

The Coach House at Dunham Massey (far left, top). The Kitchen is mainly original apart form the stone flagged-floor, which was replaced in the twentieth century. The vast aga (left) dates from 1938. A store cupboard (far left, bottom) is stocked with orginal food.

August — WEEK 32

Ada rang

1 Monday — We came away from the Hotel called in Lincoln it was very hot again got home around 6 Ray, Mike, Ada rang
Summer Bank Holiday, Scotland
Holiday, Republic of Ireland
First Day of Ramadān (subject to sighting of the moon)

2 Tuesday — I did the washing Jim went to the Town centre, I did the ironing then we went to Stockton got a top

3 Wednesday — went to Stocktons Jim came but he didnt get any chicken got a blouse Aunt Ada and I went to the church for a cuppa then went to our Adas good time

4 Thursday — Mike came over went to the Gate with Dad. We all got the bus Mike to M.Bro us to Stockton Michael rang before we went out.

5 Friday — We went to Hartlepool I got some step props and a blouse Michael phoned he's at a wedding.

6 Saturday — I went to Stocktons Jim went to the Town centre we went to the club Sue wasn't out
First Quarter

7 Sunday — We went to Stockton Mike rang while out he phoned again twice

WEEK 33 Carl phoned Leah rang **August**

Monday 8
We had a walk down the village. Leah phoned. Carl phoned went to the club. Leah rang

Tuesday 9
we went to Stockton Michael phoned twice we went to the club down the dance hall

Wednesday 10
went to pick my tablets then we went to M.Bro. then up to see Mike we came home stayed in

Thursday 11
Mike came gone to the club with his dad. after Mike went we went to Stockton I bought a top. Mike rang.

Friday 12
Mike rang I cut Jim's hair we cleaned up then went to Stockton Jim booked a trip for 9th Sep for my birthday.

Full Moon / **Saturday 13**
we got the bus together Jim to Norton me to Stockton we seen Maria rang Ada she rang back Mike rang twice we went to the club.

Sunday 14
we went to Stockton Michael phoned Carl phoned 29 vs since he met Heidi

August

WEEK 34

15 Monday We went over the Town Centre seen Dave and Maria called in the Forum it looks good

16 Tuesday Michael phoned Jim phoned him back we went to Stockton we went to the Club we went down the dance hall

17 Wednesday Met Aunt Ada in Stockton Jim came with me his going to see about the hob he got £9 off when he went.

18 Thursday Michael phoned his coming over then went to the Club to play snooker the score is 1 all went to the club.

19 Friday Did the sheets and towels got them all dry, then we went to Stockton, went to the Club came home early

20 Saturday we got the toys together Jim to Norton me to Stockton Mike rang Jim rang Mike Michael rang after my bath

21 Sunday Mike rang twice we went down Tesco's even got some apples + Apricots off the bye pass trees rang three more times

Blackberry Tea Bread

Made with freshly harvested hedgerow berries, this tea loaf from Trelissick in Cornwall makes a delicious change from more traditional fruited breads and is a great way of making the most of the blackberries that flourish in our hedgerows every summer.

Makes 1 x 900g (2lb) loaf
350g (12oz) plain flour, sifted
1 tsp mixed spice
175g (6oz) butter, softened
175g (6oz) caster sugar
225g (8oz) fresh or frozen blackberries (if frozen, use straight from the freezer)
grated rind and juice of 1 lemon
1 tbsp black treacle
2 eggs, beaten
1/2 tsp bicarbonate of soda
2 tbsp milk

Preheat the oven to 180°C, 350°F, gas mark 4. Grease and line a 900g (2lb) loaf tin. Mix together the flour and mixed spice and rub in the butter until the mixture bears a resemblance to fine breadcrumbs. Add the sugar, blackberries, lemon rind and juice, treacle and eggs and mix well. Dissolve the bicarbonate of soda in the milk, add to the mixture and beat well. Pour into the prepared tin, level and bake for 45 minutes. Reduce the oven temperature to 150°C, 300°F, gas mark 2 and cook for a further 30-45 minutes until a skewer comes out clean. Remove from the oven and leave in the tin for about 15 minutes before turning out on to a wire rack to cool.

WEEK 35 — August

Carl rang missed W Wishy me.

Monday 22
We went to Stockton I paid
my phone bill Mike rang I missed
him so I rang him back. Aunt Ada
rang went to the club

Tuesday 23
Michael phoned. Jims gone to Norton
I'm staying in went to the Club
had a good time Sue was out

Wednesday 24
Met Aunt Ada in Stockton we
had a look round then went for a
cuppa in the church.

Thursday 25
Michael came over went to the club
to play snooker. with his Dad
the score was 2 nil to Jims.

Friday 26
Jim went to Norton I stayed in
did the housework Michael
phoned twice upto now.

Saturday 27
We went to Stockton Michael
phoned twice and again Carl
never phoned don't know way.

Sunday 28
Mike rang went to the Asda, got
some bargains + Wishy We missed
Carls phone call

Erddig

Wrexham, North Wales

Erddig Apple Scones

This recipe comes from Erddig where apple scones are served with Welsh cheese. Each year the estate holds an Apple Day, when the head gardener puts on a display of the old apple species grown in the garden. There is a demonstration of cider-making by one of the Bulmer family, and cider is available to drink. You can buy apples direct from the growers and original pictures of apples direct from artists.

Makes 12 scones
450g (1lb) self-raising flour
1 tsp salt
110g (4oz) butter
50g (2oz) caster sugar
450g (1lb) dessert apples
milk to mix

Preheat oven to 200°C, 400°F, gas mark 6. Grease and flour a baking sheet. Sieve the flour and salt into a large bowl. Cut the butter into small pieces and rub into the flour until the mixture resembles coarse breadcrumbs. Stir in caster sugar. Peel and core the apples, grate half and roughly chop the rest. Stir into the mixture. Add sufficient milk to make a soft dough. Turn it onto a floured board. Knead for a couple of minutes, then either cut into 12 or form into two soft rounds. If you choose rounds, then score each into 6 wedges. Brush the tops with milk, sprinkle with a little sugar and bake for approximately 20 minutes.

The New Kitchen (far left, bottom) at Erddig built in the early 1770s. The brass servants' bells hang above their designated room plaque (far left, top). (Left) A window in the cusped gable wall next to the Parterre.

August • September Carol rang   2 fim Jimmy   WEEK 36

29 Monday
New Moon
Summer Bank Holiday, UK (exc. Scotland)

After I cleaned up we went to Stockton we seen Joan Lawlor on the bus coming home.

30 Tuesday
We went to Metro only to Sainsburys rang Mike he rang back went to the Club good Night

31 Wednesday
Michael Phoned we went to Stockton seen Derinda on the bus coming home. Michael phoned stayed in

1 Thursday
Mike came over went to the Club with his dad. We went to the Club John + Val + her Sisters Iris and Bob

2 Friday
We went to Stockton Mike rang twice we went to the club Not many in talked to Ann Marie

3 Saturday
I went to Stockton Jim went to Town. Seen Jeff and also Maria Carol rang Nathaneal moving to Mexico

4 Sunday
First Quarter
Father's Day, Australia and New Zealand

We went to Stockton after I had done the bedding Mike rang while we were out

Freshly picked vegetables in the garden at Knightshayes Court, Tiverton, Devon.

September 9th Folkstone   WEEK 37

5 Monday Jim went to pick up his ~~teeth~~ pills then after lunch we went to Stockton & went for my pills

6 Tuesday Michael phoned Jim's gone to Nortons. I'm having a lazy day Mike rang twice more. Aunt Ada rang

7 Wednesday Met Aunt Ada in Stockton Jim went to Marks went to the church for a cuppa

8 Thursday Mike rang he came over went to the sons with Dad he bought me a nice shoping bag went to Stan got a jeans

9 Friday We went to Stockton to pick up the coach to Folkstone the bus was spot on time we arrived about 4.30 unpacked then went down stairs

10 Saturday We went on the Ferry to France got my cigs good smooth passage

11 Sunday we went to the shops then got the bus to Hytchurch we had a good day out for my Birthday

WEEK 38 — September

£10 on my phone Carol sent a card I got 2 wickys

Full Moon — Monday 12
We left the hotel at 8 o'clock got home at 4:30 Ada rang twice so I rang her also Michael.

Tuesday 13
We went to Stockton got my phone toped up. We went to the club down the dance hall

Wednesday 14
Mike rang we went to M'bro I got two wickys came home went to the club down the Dance hall

Thursday 15
Jim + Mike peausied snooker After Mike went we went over the Town centre Jim got Bottles

Friday 16
We went to Stockton got a top + trouser for Jim 3 thing for the stairs Jim got a rug went to the club

Saturday 17
I went to Stockton didn't buy a lot seen Jeff at the bus stop Michael rang while out

Sunday 18
I did the washing then we went to Stockton. Carl phoned.

September — WEEK 39

Tracy 2-15
Jim did my hair

19 Monday
I went to see Tracy my Blood Pressure is O.K. We went to the Club

20 Tuesday — Last Quarter
We went to Stockton Jim did my hair. it looks good went to the club

21 Wednesday
Met Aunt Ada in Stockton came home Jim and I went to Hartlepool stayed in

22 Thursday
We went to Stockton went to the Club Bob + Jim John + Val and Vals two sisters were out

23 Friday — Autumnal Equinox (Autumn begins)
We went to Stockton didn't get any chicken. Went to the club no one in hardly

24 Saturday
Jim went to the Town centre I cleaned up. Then we went to the Cons down the dance hall

25 Sunday
We got the coach went to Bolton nice hotel

Golden Cider Soup

This recipe comes from Montacute, Somerset, a glorious, golden house set in lush countryside of orchards and green fields, so use Somerset cider for preference. The cider gives this simple recipe a wonderful luxurious flavour. The soup can be served hot or cold – it is equally delicious either way. It is best very smooth – even though pushing a soup through a sieve is tedious – the result is rewarding.

Serves 6
50g (2oz) butter
225g (8oz) carrots, diced
225g (8oz) potatoes, diced
2 garlic cloves, crushed
400g tin chopped tomatoes
450ml (3/4 pint) medium or sweet cider
450ml (3/4 pint) vegetable stock

For Garnish
salt and freshly ground black pepper to taste
crème fraîche
basil leaves

Melt the butter in a large saucepan and sweat the diced carrots and potatoes for 5 minutes. Add the crushed garlic, tin of tomatoes, cider and vegetable stock and bring to the boil. Cover and simmer until the vegetables are tender. Season with salt and pepper. Pour into a food processor and blend until very smooth. Then press the mixture through a sieve before returning it to the pan and reheating before serving. Garnish each bowl with a spoonful of crème fraîche and a couple of basil leaves.

WEEK 40

September • October

Monday 26
We went down the Castle for our dinners then watched the lights very good.

Tuesday 27 — New Moon
Jims birthday we went to Southport got some slippers for pants and a watch for me

Wednesday 28
We called at the Trafford Centre on the way got in Stockton around 4.30. rang Aunt Ada

Thursday 29 — Michaelmas Day / Jewish New Year (Rosh Hashanah)
Michael phoned he's at Redcar I woke up with my leg hurting did the washing + ironing then we went to Stockton

Friday 30
rang Mike we went to Stockton Carl rang went to the club Sue was in Mike rang again

Saturday 1
I went to Stockton Mike rang while out We went to the cong Sue was in hasn't been in for 4 weeks

Sunday 2
Mike rang. We went to m Bro to see him he was in a nasty mood we seen Graham

Oxburgh Hall

Oxborough, Norfolk

Piccalilli

'*Take vinegar one gallon, garlic one pound, ginger one pound, turmeric, mustard seed, long pepper and salt of each 4 ounces.*' These are some of the ingredients for an Indian pickle written down in 1765. By this time the East India Company had familiarized the well-off with *chatnis* from the East. In Piccalilli the mustard acts as a preservative as well as the vinegar. This recipe comes from Oxburgh Hall where they pickle seasonal vegetables from their kitchen garden.

Makes approximately 6 jars

2.75kg (6lb) prepared vegetables (a mixture of diced cucumber, marrow, courgette, beans, cauliflower florets and small onions)
450g (1lb) cooking salt
25-40g (1-1½oz) mustard powder
25-40g (1-1½oz) ground ginger
175g (6oz) white sugar
1 litre (2 pints) distilled malt vinegar
20g (¾oz) cornflour
15g (½oz) ground turmeric

Layer the prepared vegetables on a large plate with the salt and leave overnight covered with a cloth. Next day, drain and rinse the vegetables under cold running water, then dry well. Stir the mustard, ginger and sugar into most of the vinegar, retaining just enough to make a thin paste with the cornflour and turmeric. Add the vegetables and simmer until you have a texture you like; crisp or less crisp, your choice. Add the cornflour and turmeric paste to the pan. Bring to the boil, stirring carefully, and boil for 2-3 minutes. Pour into warm jars and cover with a cloth. Leave until completely cold, then seal. Store for 2-3 months before using.

The north-west corner of Oxburgh Hall seen from across the moat (far left, bottom). The towers of the Gatehouse rise up from the water beside the bridge. (Left) The herbaceous border in the garden.

October

Rang Ada
Rang Carl

WEEK 41

3 Monday
Mike rang Jim went to Stockton we went to Argos and bought a washer mine broke

4 Tuesday
We went to Stockton I bought Kettle and a Toaster phoned Ada rang Mike he was waiting for a call

First Quarter

5 Wednesday
I went to meet Aunt Ada at Stockton then I went back to hers then Ada picked me up and went to hers.

6 Thursday
Mike rang he peepled in went to the Club with his dad We went to Stockton and the Club

7 Friday
I went to get my ears tested on my own. Then Jim went to the Town Centre

8 Saturday
The chap came with the Washing I went to Stockton Cleaned the cubards out. Mike rang

Day of Atonement (Yom Kippur)

9 Sunday
We went to the Asda and I packed for hol

WEEK 42 — **October**

Monday 10 — Holiday, USA (Columbus Day) / Holiday, Canada (Thanksgiving)

We went to Stockton the bus was on time we had a good run down.

Tuesday 11

We went to John Lennon airport it was about a hour away on the bus.

Wednesday 12 — Full Moon

We went to Aintree race course and went to the railway station the race course was very good

---

Thursday 13 — First Day of Tabernacles (Succoth)

We went round Liverpool and had a look in all the big shops

Friday 14

We got the bus to come home at 1 o'clock got home around 5-30 went to the club

---

Saturday 15

Jim went to Stockton then I went later on.

Sunday 16

We went to Stockton Mike rang after I rang him we did the Bkitchen drawsi out

October

Hair cut I paid £7-50

WEEK 43

17 Monday We went to Stockton & rang Mike after he had rang me. he rang his dad. Went to the club.

18 Tuesday We went to Stockton to sort out my bank went to the club phoned Carl when we came home

19 Wednesday Met Aunt Ada at Stockton we went shopping then went for a cuppa in the church

20 Thursday Jim went to the Town Centre after Mike had gone Aunt Ada rang but I didn't get her what she wanted went to the club. *Last Quarter*

21 Friday Sue came and cut our hair we went to Stockton went to the club. came home early

22 Saturday I went to Stockton Jim went to Norton we went to the club but came home early Michael phoned when we got home

23 Sunday We went to Stockton Mike rang we did the windows Jim rang Michael

Hardwick Hall, seen through the orchard planted with traditional varieties of apple and pear trees.

Pear and Rosemary Jelly

Ellen Jefferies is famous at Erddig, North Wales for her spiced jelly preserves using fruits from the garden, orchard and hedgerow and either fresh herbs or spices from the store cupboard. This recipe makes a wonderful alternative to the more common apple jelly.

Makes about 8 small jars
900g (2lb) pears
pared zest and juice of 2 lemons
large bunch of rosemary
sugar, granulated or preserving
225ml (8fl oz) pectin, if necessary

This recipe takes two days to make. Put the pears, rosemary, lemon zest and juice in a preserving pan. Add sufficient water to cover them. Cover the pan and simmer until the fruit is very soft. This should take around 30 minutes. Strain through a jelly bag overnight.

The next day, measure the juice into a clean preserving pan. Add 450g (1lb) sugar for each 600ml (1 pint) of juice. Heat gently until the sugar has dissolved, then boil rapidly until setting point is reached, stirring from time to time. (Add the pectin at the end if it is difficult to get the jelly to set.) Skim, pour the jelly into warm jars and cover. Seal when still hot.

October

WEEK 44

I got the washing

Monday 24 — Holiday, New Zealand (Labour Day) / United Nations Day
I did some washing cleared the nick nacks out of the bedroom Mike rang missed the call

Tuesday 25
Went to Stockton got some chicken seen Joan Lawts on the bus allso Duncan Mike rang

Wednesday 26 — New Moon
We went to Stockton got some lights got my new bank book Michael rang.

Thursday 27
Michael came went club Score 1-1 We won £25 on the tickets went to Norton

Friday 28
Mike rang Jim Stockton me chemist Mike rang twice more

Saturday 29
We went to Stockton seen Mavis Michael rang he'd been to Witton with Tony

Sunday 30 — British Summer Time ends
Mike rang went to the Asda got washing

Canons Ashby House

Daventry, Northamptonshire

Canons Ashby Coconut Cake
Canons Ashby was once famous for its local postman who doubled as a hedge-clipper. One day when the owner, Sir Henry Dryden, was having a tea party on the lawn with his friends, he asked the postman to clip the yew trees while he was on the premises. As the guests watched him clip away, they decided to ask him to exercise his skills and give them each a haircut and, having performed the task to their satisfaction, he joined the tea party!

Makes 12 fingers
For the Cake
100g (4oz) butter, softened
75g (3oz) light soft brown sugar
2 tsp almond essence
grated rind of 1 lemon
1 egg, beaten
250g (9oz) plain flour, sifted
5–6 tbsp plum jam

For the Topping
1 egg, beaten
75g (3oz) light soft brown sugar
100g (4oz) shredded coconut

For Dipping
175–225g (6–8oz) milk or plain chocolate

Preheat the oven to 180°C, 350°F, gas mark 4. Grease a 17.5 x 27.5cm (7 x 11in) Swiss roll tin. Beat together the butter, sugar, almond essence, lemon rind and egg. Add the flour and mix well. Press into the prepared tin and spread a layer of jam on top. Mix together the ingredients for the topping and spread over the jam. Bake for 20–30 minutes until firm and pale golden. Remove from the oven and leave to cool in the tin. When cold, cut into fingers and lift carefully from the tin. Melt the chocolate and dip both ends of each finger into it. Place carefully on a wire rack to set.

The south front of Canons Ashby (far left, top). (Far left, bottom and left) The Kitchen with its stone flagged floor, cast iron range, cooking utensils and servants' bells.

Elida rang Scarbrough 5 days

October • November — WEEK 45

31 Monday — Hallowe'en / Holiday, Republic of Ireland

1 Tuesday — All Saints' Day

2 Wednesday — First Quarter

3 Thursday

Scarbrough

4 Friday

home

5 Saturday — Guy Fawkes' Day

Cath rang Elida rang Ada + Michael also

6 Sunday

We went to the Ada Mike rang about 4 times

WEEK 46 — Carol rang — November

Monday 7
Jim went to Stockton got me a Jacket Mike rang his going to a show tonight

Tuesday 8
Michael phoned I rang Aunt Ada she's not going to Stockton she's getting her feet done went to the Club

Wednesday 9
We went to Stockton seen Mavis at the bus stop Michael phoned twice.

Thursday 10 — Full Moon
I met Aunt Ada in Midlesbrough and I seen Mike at the bus station

Friday 11 — Holiday, USA (Veterans' Day) / Holiday, Canada (Remembrance Day)
Jim went T. centre I rang Mike we went to Stockton only got shoping went to the Club

Saturday 12
went to Ston gim shops Mike rang I rang him Carol rang Mike again same time as Carol went to the club.

Sunday 13 — Remembrance Sunday, UK
Jim not well I done the china cabenet out and did some washing Mike rang twice

November — WEEK 47

rang Carl 11th no answer

14 Monday We got the bus to Stockton ~~...~~ called in at the War Museum.

15 Tuesday I went to Stockton to pay for my bill. Then I went over the doctors with Jim. Elsida phoned when we got home.

16 Wednesday I got the Wedding photos at last. Went to Stockton sent Tiffany card Aunt Ada phoned rang Carl.

17 Thursday I met Aunt Ada in Stockton we got some chicken so did she went in the church for a cuppa

18 Friday *Last Quarter* — I went over the chemist for my tablets. Jim went to the Town Centre.

19 Saturday We both went to Stockton Carl phoned we went to the club

20 Sunday We stayed in all day to relax I phoned Michael he rang me later.

Christmas Pudding

Plum Pudding, as this used to be called, has been associated with Christmas only since Prince Albert, Queen Victoria's husband, introduced it. The making and the eating of Christmas pudding has become thick with tradition. It should be made on Stir-Up Sunday, the Sunday before Advent, and all the family should give it a stir and make a wish. Silver coins – these used to be silver threepenny pieces – are cooked with the pudding, as are charms. The various charms have significance. A ring means marriage; a horseshoe is good luck.

Makes 2 puddings serving 6 or 1 large pudding serving 12
225g (8oz) raisins
175g (6oz) sultanas
175g (6oz) currants
50g (2oz) candied peel
25g (1oz) flaked almonds
25g (1oz) flour
1 tsp mixed spice
1 tsp cinnamon
1/2 tsp nutmeg
110g (4oz) caster sugar
110g (4oz) fresh white breadcrumbs
grated zest and juice of 1 lemon
25g (1oz) butter
2 eggs
150ml (1/4 pint) orange juice

In a large bowl mix together the raisins, sultanas, currants, candied peel and almonds. Sieve the flour with the mixed spice, cinnamon and nutmeg. Add to the fruit, together with the sugar and breadcrumbs, grated zest and juice of the lemon, and the diced butter. Mix thoroughly. Beat the eggs well with the orange juice and stir into the mixture. Leave to stand overnight.

The next day, pack the mixture into pudding basins. There is probably sufficient mixture for one large or two medium-sized basins. Leave at least 2.5cm (1in) at the top for expansion. Cover with greaseproof paper and foil and tuck it down round the rim. Stand the basins on top of the upturned saucers in a pan. Fill the pan with water to halfway up the basins and simmer for at least 3 hours.

The puddings will keep for as many months as you want. They taste just as good even a year later. On Christmas Day, re-cover with fresh paper and foil and steam for an hour before serving.

November

WEEK 48 — 2 Wks to go — Mce 22 Nov.

Monday 21
We went to Stockton & paid my telephone bill Michael called after we got home.

Tuesday 22
Went to M.Bro' & got 3 bottles of plonk phoned Aunt Ada she's not very well

Wednesday 23
we went to Stockton seen Norm and Benny in Stockton Michael phoned when we got home

Thursday 24
Holiday, USA (Thanksgiving Day)
Michael came had some photos Carl had sent him he went to see Duncan at 1-15

Friday 25
New Moon
we went to Stockton Mike had phoned while we were out but he ~~was~~ got us later

Saturday 26
Jim went to Norton I cleaned up and down its very cold and windy so I didn't go to Stockton.

Sunday 27
First Sunday in Advent
Islamic New Year (subject to sighting of the moon)
We went to Stockton Michael phoned

Blue and white ceramic flatware in the Dining Room at Smallhythe Place, Kent. This was the home Ellen Terry, the actress, from 1899 to 1928.

Buckland Abbey

Yelverton, Devon

Mulled Wine

This particular mull is rather like hot sangria – rather appropriate as the recipe comes from Buckland Abbey, the home of Sir Frances Drake, commander of the English fleet that defeated the Spanish Armada in 1688.

Makes 6-8 glasses
1 orange
12-14 whole cloves
1 litre (1³/₄ pints) red wine
1 litre (1³/₄ pints) lemonade
50g (2oz) brown sugar
150ml (1/4 pint) orange juice
1 cinnamon stick 15cm (6in) long

Stud the orange with the cloves and cut in half. Place all the ingredients in a large pan and bring very slowly almost to a simmer. Serve hot but do not allow to boil.

View through to the Herb Garden at Buckland Abbey (far left, top). The sixteenth-century kitchen (left) was built by Sir Richard Grenville. The kitchen is dominated by two open hearths used for cooking, with roasting spits stored above. A dresser in the kitchen displays blue and white china (far left, bottom).

November • December

WEEK 49

Monday 28
We went to Hartlepool after Lunch phoned Michael he phoned me back.

Tuesday 29
We went to Midlesbrough very cold and Windy Michael rang Elida phoned him up

Wednesday 30 — St. Andrew's Day
Met Aunt Ada at Stockton Jim came on the bus with me but he didn't stay while we went shopping

Thursday 1
Michael came over its very cold they didn't go to the club for a game of snooker.

Friday 2 — First Quarter
We went to Stockton we got some chicken Michael phoned

Saturday 3
Jim went Town Center I went to Stockton very cold.

Sunday 4
We went to Manchester Elida came we had a good Natter Lovely to see her.

The Wedgwood breakfast service in the China Room at Penrhyn Castle, Gwynedd.

December Phoned Carol.

WEEK 50

5 Monday Went to the Market but came back on the Bus.

6 Tuesday Came home got home around 2-30 Went to the Club

7 Wednesday Met Aunt Ada in Stockton very cold and windy

8 Thursday We went to see Michael went to the Club, Bob + Iris + John + Val were in.

9 Friday Jim went to the shops I cleaned up we went to the Club.

10 Saturday We went to Stockton & got two Diarys for us. *Full Moon*

11 Sunday Went to Stockton Jim got me a black top and a pair of brown shoes

WEEK 51 Jims did my hair — **December**

Monday 12
Jim went to Stockton
I washed ~~today~~ ironed and
hovered up Mike rang twice

Tuesday 13
Jim went to the Shops
I stayed home we went to
the Club.

Wednesday 14
we went to Stockton
Mike phoned twice

Thursday 15
We went to Stockton Mike
Jim did my hair I
phoned Michael came

Friday 16
We went to Stockton
Went to the club
I rang Mike

Saturday 17

Last Quarter

Sunday 18

December

WEEK 52

19 Monday

20 Tuesday

21 Wednesday

22 Thursday   Winter Solstice (Winter begins)

23 Friday

24 Saturday   *New Moon*
                                                                                    Christmas Eve

25 Sunday   Christmas Day

                                                                  Christmas baking in the kitchen
                                                                       at Petworth, West Sussex.

Ripon Christmas Bread

In most areas of Britain in the past, large batches of fruit loaves were baked at Christmas ready to feed the family and any visitors who called at the house between Christmas and New Year. This festive loaf from Yorkshire is a traditional enriched bread dough which includes allspice in the ingredients. Also called Jamaican Pepper or newspice, it is the dried unripe fruit of *Pimenta dioica* plant. Its aroma and taste combines the complex characters of cinnamon and cloves and adds a slightly hotter, peppery quality.

Makes 2 x 900g (2lb) loaves
For the basic bread dough
900g (2lb) plain flour sifted
2 tsp salt
25g (1oz) fresh yeast
1 tsp caster sugar
100g (4oz) butter, softened
600ml (1 pint) milk, warmed

For the additional flavouring
175g (6oz) lard, softened and cut into small pieces
100g (4oz) raisins
50g (2oz) mixed candied peel
100g (4oz) granulated or caster sugar
225g (8oz) currants
1/2 tsp allspice

First make the basic bread dough. Mix together the flour and salt. Cream the yeast with the sugar. Rub the fat into the flour, add the yeast and warm milk and mix to a light dough. Knead well with floured hands until smooth. Place the dough in a bowl and stand in a warm place for 1½–2 hours until doubled in size. Grease two 900g (2lb) loaf tins. Mix together all the additional ingredients and work into the dough until all are evenly distributed. Divide the mixture between the tins and leave in a warm place until the dough almost reaches the top of the tins. Meanwhile heat the oven to 160°C, 325°F, gas mark 3. When the loaves are well risen, bake for approximately 2 hours until golden and firm. Remove from the oven and turn out on to a wire rack to cool. Serve either warm or cold and spread with butter.

WEEK 53

December • January 2012

Monday 26

Boxing Day (St. Stephen's Day)
Holiday, UK, Republic of Ireland, USA, Canada, Australia and New Zealand

Tuesday 27

Holiday, UK, Australia and New Zealand

Wednesday 28

Thursday 29

Friday 30

Saturday 31

New Year's Eve

Sunday 1

New Year's Day

Shopping

Many of the National Trust properties have a shop on the premises but you can also shop with the National Trust at the following high street locations as well as online at www.nationaltrust.org.uk

Bath
Marshal Wades House
14 Abbey Churchyard
Bath
NE Somerset
BA1 1LY
01225 460249

Cambridge
9 Kings Parade
Cambridge
Cambridgeshire
CB2 1SJ
01223 311894

Canterbury
24 Burgate
Canterbury
Kent
CT1 2HA
01227 457120

Chichester
92a East Street
Chichester
West Sussex
PO19 1HA
01243 773125

Dartmouth
8 The Quay
Dartmouth
Devon
TQ6 9PS
01803 833694

Heelis
Kemble Drive
Swindon
Wiltshire
SN2 2NA
01793 817600

Hereford
7 Gomond Street
Hereford
HR1 2DP
01432 342297

Hexham
25-26 Market Place
Hexham
Northumberland
NE46 3PB
01434 607654

Kendal
16-20 Stricklandgate
Kendal
Cumbria
LA9 4ND
01539 736190

London
Blewcoat
23 Caxton Street
Westminster
London
SW1H 0PY
020 72222877

Monmouth
5 Church Street
Monmouth
Gwent
NP5 3BX
01600 713270

Salisbury
House Of Steps
41 High Street
Salisbury
Wiltshire
SP1 2PB
01722 331884

Sidmouth
Old Fore Street
Sidmouth
Devon
EX10 8LS
01395 578107

Skipton
6 Sheep Street
Skipton
West Yorkshire
BD23 1JH
01756 799378

Stratford
45 Wood Street
Stratford-upon-Avon
Warwickshire
CV37 6JG
01789 298158

Street Shop
Unit 44, Clarks Village
Farm Road
Street
Somerset
BA17 0BB
01789 298158

Truro
9 River Street
Truro
Cornwall
TR1 2SQ
01872 241464

Wells
16 Market Place
Wells
Somerset
BA5 2RB
01749 677735

York
Shop & Information
Centre
32 Goodramgate
York
North Yorkshire
YO1 2LG
01904 659050